45 Thanksgiving Recipes for Home

By: Kelly Johnson

Table of Contents

Appetizers:

- Stuffed Mushrooms
- Cranberry Brie Bites
- Deviled Eggs
- Spinach Artichoke Dip

Main Course - Turkey:

- Roast Turkey
- Herb-Roasted Turkey Breast
- Deep-Fried Turkey

Side Dishes:

- Mashed Potatoes
- Stuffing/Dressing
- Sweet Potato Casserole
- Green Bean Casserole
- Brussels Sprouts with Bacon

Gravy:

- Turkey Gravy

Cranberry Sauce:

- Homemade Cranberry Sauce

Breads:

- Classic Dinner Rolls
- Cornbread

Soups:

- Butternut Squash Soup
- Roasted Pumpkin Soup

Salads:

- Harvest Salad
- Cranberry Walnut Salad

Potatoes:

- Scalloped Potatoes
- Garlic Mashed Potatoes

Vegetarian Options:

- Stuffed Acorn Squash
- Vegetarian Wellington

Desserts - Pies:

- Pumpkin Pie
- Pecan Pie
- Apple Pie

Desserts - Other:

- Pumpkin Cheesecake
- Chocolate Pecan Tart

Desserts - Cookies:

- Pumpkin Snickerdoodles
- Pecan Sandies
- Thanksgiving Sugar Cookies

Desserts - Cakes:

- Apple Cider Cake
- Maple Pecan Cake

Drinks:

- Spiced Apple Cider
- Cranberry Orange Punch

Leftovers:

- Turkey Pot Pie
- Thanksgiving Leftover Sandwich

Miscellaneous:

- Homemade Grilled Turkey Stock
- Candied Sweet Potatoes

Breakfast/Brunch:

- Pumpkin Pancakes
- Thanksgiving Breakfast Casserole

Extras:

- Homemade Cranberry Butter
- Homemade Dinner Rolls
- Caramel Apple Cheesecake Bars

Appetizers:

Stuffed Mushrooms

Ingredients:

- 20 large white button mushrooms, cleaned and stems removed
- 1/2 cup Italian seasoned breadcrumbs
- 1/4 cup grated Parmesan cheese
- 1/4 cup chopped fresh parsley
- 3 cloves garlic, minced
- 1/4 cup finely chopped onion
- 3 tablespoons olive oil
- Salt and black pepper to taste
- Optional: 1/4 cup shredded mozzarella cheese for topping

Instructions:

Preheat the Oven:
- Preheat your oven to 375°F (190°C).

Prepare the Mushrooms:
- Clean the mushrooms and remove the stems. Place the mushroom caps on a baking sheet, cap side down.

Prepare the Filling:
- Chop the mushroom stems finely. In a skillet, heat olive oil over medium heat. Add chopped mushroom stems, garlic, and onions. Sauté until the vegetables are softened.

Make the Stuffing:
- In a bowl, combine the sautéed mushroom mixture with breadcrumbs, Parmesan cheese, chopped parsley, salt, and black pepper. Mix well.

Stuff the Mushrooms:
- Using a teaspoon, fill each mushroom cap with the stuffing mixture, pressing it down slightly.

Optional Cheese Topping:
- If desired, sprinkle a bit of shredded mozzarella cheese on top of each stuffed mushroom for added richness.

Bake:
- Bake the stuffed mushrooms in the preheated oven for about 15-20 minutes or until the mushrooms are tender and the tops are golden brown.

Serve Warm:
- Remove from the oven and let them cool slightly before serving. Enjoy these delicious stuffed mushrooms warm!

Tips:

- Variations: Feel free to customize the filling by adding ingredients like cooked sausage, breadcrumbs, or different herbs.
- Make-Ahead: You can prepare the stuffed mushrooms up to a day in advance, refrigerate them, and bake them just before serving.

These Stuffed Mushrooms make an excellent appetizer for Thanksgiving or any festive gathering. They are packed with savory flavors and are sure to be a hit with your guests!

Cranberry Brie Bites

Ingredients:

- 1 sheet of puff pastry, thawed
- 1/2 cup cranberry sauce (homemade or store-bought)
- 8 ounces Brie cheese, cut into small cubes
- 1 tablespoon honey
- Fresh rosemary sprigs for garnish (optional)

Instructions:

Preheat the Oven:
- Preheat your oven to 375°F (190°C).

Prepare the Puff Pastry:
- Roll out the puff pastry on a lightly floured surface. If it's not already in a sheet, you can roll it into a rectangle.

Cut into Squares:
- Cut the puff pastry into squares, approximately 2x2 inches each.

Assemble the Bites:
- Place a small cube of Brie cheese in the center of each puff pastry square. Top it with a small spoonful of cranberry sauce.

Fold and Seal:
- Fold the corners of the puff pastry squares over the Brie and cranberry, creating a little bundle. Press the edges to seal.

Place on Baking Sheet:
- Arrange the assembled Cranberry Brie Bites on a baking sheet lined with parchment paper.

Bake:
- Bake in the preheated oven for about 12-15 minutes or until the puff pastry is golden brown and puffed.

Drizzle with Honey:
- Once out of the oven, drizzle the Cranberry Brie Bites with honey for a touch of sweetness.

Garnish:
- Optionally, garnish each bite with a small sprig of fresh rosemary for a festive touch.

Serve Warm:
- Allow the Cranberry Brie Bites to cool slightly before serving. They are best enjoyed while still warm.

Tips:

- Customize: Experiment with different types of cranberry sauce (whole berry, spiced, etc.) for varied flavors.
- Add Nuts: For extra crunch, consider adding a sprinkle of chopped nuts like pecans or walnuts.

These Cranberry Brie Bites are a crowd-pleaser, combining the richness of Brie with the tangy sweetness of cranberry sauce, all wrapped in flaky puff pastry. They make a perfect appetizer for holiday gatherings and celebrations.

Deviled Eggs

Ingredients:

- 6 large eggs, hard-boiled and peeled
- 1/4 cup mayonnaise
- 1 teaspoon Dijon mustard
- 1 teaspoon white vinegar
- Salt and pepper to taste
- Paprika and chopped fresh chives for garnish

Instructions:

Hard-Boil the Eggs:
- Place the eggs in a saucepan and cover them with water. Bring to a boil, then reduce the heat and simmer for 10-12 minutes. Once done, transfer the eggs to an ice bath to cool before peeling.

Slice and Remove Yolks:
- Once the eggs are cooled and peeled, cut them in half lengthwise. Carefully remove the yolks and place them in a bowl.

Prepare the Filling:
- Mash the egg yolks with a fork. Add mayonnaise, Dijon mustard, white vinegar, salt, and pepper. Mix until smooth and well combined.

Fill the Egg Whites:
- Spoon or pipe the yolk mixture back into the egg white halves, creating a little mound.

Garnish:
- Sprinkle each deviled egg with a pinch of paprika and chopped fresh chives for added flavor and a pop of color.

Chill:
- Refrigerate the deviled eggs for at least 30 minutes before serving to allow the flavors to meld.

Serve:
- Arrange the deviled eggs on a serving platter and serve chilled.

Tips:

- Piping Bag: For a neater presentation, you can use a piping bag to fill the egg whites with the yolk mixture.

- Variations: Get creative with your filling by adding ingredients like diced pickles, horseradish, or a dash of hot sauce for extra flavor.

Deviled eggs are a classic, crowd-pleasing appetizer that's easy to make and always a hit at gatherings. They're perfect for any occasion, including Thanksgiving and other holidays.

Spinach Artichoke Dip

Ingredients:

- 1 (10-ounce) package frozen chopped spinach, thawed and drained
- 1 (14-ounce) can artichoke hearts, drained and chopped
- 1/2 cup mayonnaise
- 1/2 cup sour cream
- 1 cup grated Parmesan cheese
- 1 cup shredded mozzarella cheese
- 1 teaspoon minced garlic
- 1/2 teaspoon onion powder
- Salt and black pepper to taste
- 1/4 teaspoon crushed red pepper flakes (optional, for a bit of heat)
- Tortilla chips, bread, or vegetables for serving

Instructions:

Preheat the Oven:
- Preheat your oven to 375°F (190°C).

Prepare Spinach and Artichokes:
- Thaw the frozen chopped spinach and squeeze out any excess water. Chop the drained artichoke hearts into smaller pieces.

Mix Ingredients:
- In a large mixing bowl, combine the chopped spinach, chopped artichokes, mayonnaise, sour cream, grated Parmesan cheese, shredded mozzarella cheese, minced garlic, onion powder, salt, black pepper, and optional crushed red pepper flakes. Mix well until all ingredients are thoroughly combined.

Transfer to Baking Dish:
- Transfer the mixture to a baking dish, spreading it out evenly.

Bake:
- Bake in the preheated oven for 25-30 minutes or until the dip is hot and bubbly, and the top is golden brown.

Serve Warm:
- Remove from the oven and let it cool for a few minutes before serving. The dip is best served warm.

Serve with Accompaniments:
- Serve the Spinach Artichoke Dip with tortilla chips, slices of bread, or fresh vegetable sticks.

Tips:

- Variations: Consider adding a layer of shredded mozzarella on top before baking for an extra cheesy finish.
- Make-Ahead: You can prepare the dip up to a day in advance, cover it, and refrigerate. Bake just before serving.

Spinach Artichoke Dip is a classic party favorite, and its creamy, cheesy goodness makes it a perfect appetizer for Thanksgiving or any festive gathering.

Main Course - Turkey:

Roast Turkey

Ingredients:

- 1 whole turkey (12-15 pounds), thawed if frozen
- Salt and black pepper to taste
- 1 cup (2 sticks) unsalted butter, softened
- 1 tablespoon chopped fresh herbs (rosemary, thyme, sage)
- 1 onion, quartered
- 1 lemon, halved
- 4-6 garlic cloves, peeled
- 2 cups chicken or turkey broth
- Optional: Stuffing ingredients (such as celery, carrots, onions, fresh herbs)

Instructions:

Preheat the Oven:
- Preheat your oven to 325°F (163°C).

Prepare the Turkey:
- Remove the turkey from its packaging. Pat it dry with paper towels, inside and out.

Season the Turkey:
- Season the inside cavity of the turkey with salt and black pepper.

Optional: Stuff the Turkey:
- If you're stuffing the turkey, prepare the stuffing mixture and loosely stuff the cavity. Do not overpack as it can affect the cooking time.

Prepare the Herb Butter:
- In a small bowl, mix together the softened butter and chopped fresh herbs.

Rub Herb Butter:
- Rub the herb butter mixture all over the outside of the turkey, including under the skin if possible.

Add Aromatics:
- Place the quartered onion, halved lemon, and garlic cloves inside the turkey cavity.

Tie Legs:
- If the turkey legs are not already tied, use kitchen twine to tie them together.

Place in Roasting Pan:
- Place the turkey on a rack in a roasting pan, breast side up.

Add Broth:
- Pour the chicken or turkey broth into the bottom of the roasting pan. This helps keep the turkey moist and adds flavor to the drippings.

Cover with Foil:
- Tent the turkey with foil, leaving some space between the foil and the turkey to allow for air circulation.

Roast:
- Roast the turkey in the preheated oven. As a general rule, calculate about 15-20 minutes of cooking time per pound. Baste the turkey with pan juices every 30 minutes.

Check Temperature:
- Use a meat thermometer to check the internal temperature. The turkey is done when the thickest part of the thigh reaches 165°F (74°C). Also, check the temperature in the thickest part of the breast without touching the bone.

Rest:
- Once done, let the turkey rest for at least 20-30 minutes before carving. This allows the juices to redistribute and results in a juicier turkey.

Carve and Serve:
- Carve the turkey and serve it with your favorite Thanksgiving sides.

Tips:

- Brining: Consider brining the turkey before roasting for added flavor and moisture.
- Gravy: Use the drippings from the roasting pan to make a delicious turkey gravy.

Roasting a turkey takes time and attention, but the result is a flavorful and tender centerpiece for your Thanksgiving table. Adjust cooking times based on the size of your turkey and the accuracy of your oven.

Herb-Roasted Turkey Breast

Ingredients:

- 1 whole turkey breast (bone-in or boneless, about 5-7 pounds)
- 1/2 cup unsalted butter, softened
- 2 tablespoons chopped fresh herbs (such as rosemary, thyme, sage, and parsley)
- 4 garlic cloves, minced
- Salt and black pepper to taste
- 1 onion, sliced
- 1 carrot, chopped
- 1 celery stalk, chopped
- 1 cup chicken or turkey broth

Instructions:

Preheat the Oven:
- Preheat your oven to 325°F (163°C).

Prepare the Turkey Breast:
- Pat the turkey breast dry with paper towels. If the turkey breast has skin, gently lift it and loosen it from the meat without removing it.

Season with Herbed Butter:
- In a small bowl, mix the softened butter, chopped fresh herbs, minced garlic, salt, and black pepper. Rub this herb butter mixture all over the turkey breast, including under the skin if it's still attached.

Prepare the Roasting Pan:
- Place the sliced onion, chopped carrot, and celery in the bottom of a roasting pan. This creates a flavorful base for the turkey.

Place Turkey on Rack:
- If you have a roasting rack, place it over the vegetables in the pan. Put the turkey breast on top of the rack.

Add Broth:
- Pour the chicken or turkey broth into the bottom of the roasting pan to prevent the vegetables from burning and to create a moist cooking environment.

Roast:
- Roast the turkey breast in the preheated oven. Calculate approximately 15-20 minutes of cooking time per pound. Baste the turkey with pan juices every 30 minutes.

Check Temperature:

- Use a meat thermometer to check the internal temperature. The turkey breast is done when it reaches 165°F (74°C) in the thickest part.

Rest:
- Let the turkey breast rest for about 10-15 minutes before carving. This allows the juices to redistribute.

Carve and Serve:
- Carve the turkey breast into slices and serve with your favorite sides.

Tips:

- Herb Variations: Experiment with different herb combinations, such as adding a touch of lemon zest or using fresh oregano.
- Customize Vegetables: You can add other vegetables like potatoes, parsnips, or leeks to the roasting pan for added flavor.

This Herb-Roasted Turkey Breast is a flavorful and easy-to-make alternative to a whole turkey, making it perfect for smaller gatherings or when you prefer white meat. Enjoy your delicious and herb-infused roast!

Deep-Fried Turkey

Ingredients:

- 1 whole turkey (10-15 pounds)
- Peanut oil (or another high smoke-point oil) for frying
- Seasonings for the turkey (dry rub or injectable marinade)
- Salt and black pepper to taste

Instructions:

Important Note: Deep-frying a turkey requires special equipment, and it should be done outdoors in a safe and controlled environment. Follow all safety guidelines provided with your fryer, and never use it indoors or under a covered area.

Prepare the Turkey:
- Ensure the turkey is completely thawed and dry. Remove any packaging, and pat it dry with paper towels.

Season the Turkey:
- Season the turkey with your preferred dry rub or injectable marinade. Ensure it's seasoned both inside and out.

Prepare the Fryer:
- Set up your outdoor propane deep fryer on a flat surface away from structures, trees, and other flammable items. Follow the manufacturer's instructions for your specific fryer.

Add Oil:
- Fill the fryer with the appropriate amount of oil, following the manufacturer's guidelines. The oil level should be sufficient to fully immerse the turkey but not overflow when the turkey is added.

Preheat the Oil:
- Heat the oil to the desired temperature (usually around 350°F or 175°C). Use a reliable thermometer to monitor the oil temperature.

Prepare for Frying:
- Make sure the turkey is at room temperature. Pat it dry one more time if needed.

Lower the Turkey:
- Slowly and carefully lower the turkey into the hot oil using the provided basket or a turkey rack.

Fry the Turkey:
- Fry the turkey for about 3-4 minutes per pound. The internal temperature should reach 165°F (74°C) in the thickest part of the turkey.

Remove and Drain:
- Once the turkey reaches the desired temperature, carefully lift it out of the oil and allow it to drain on paper towels or a wire rack.

Rest and Carve:
- Let the deep-fried turkey rest for about 20 minutes before carving.

Safety Tips:

- Outdoor Use Only: Never use a turkey fryer indoors or under a covered area.
- Dry Turkey: Ensure the turkey is completely dry before frying to prevent oil splatters.
- Follow Manufacturer's Instructions: Always follow the guidelines provided by the turkey fryer manufacturer.

Deep-fried turkey can be a delicious and unique option for your Thanksgiving meal, but safety is of utmost importance. Exercise caution, follow the instructions provided with your fryer, and enjoy your crispy and flavorful turkey!

Side Dishes:

Mashed Potatoes

Ingredients:

- 4 pounds Russet or Yukon Gold potatoes, peeled and cut into chunks
- 1 cup whole milk or heavy cream
- 1/2 cup unsalted butter
- Salt, to taste
- Black pepper, to taste
- Optional: Chopped fresh chives or parsley for garnish

Instructions:

Boil the Potatoes:
- Place the peeled and chopped potatoes in a large pot of cold, salted water. Bring to a boil and cook until the potatoes are fork-tender, about 15-20 minutes.

Drain the Potatoes:
- Drain the potatoes in a colander and return them to the pot. Allow any excess water to evaporate.

Heat the Milk (or Cream):
- In a small saucepan, heat the milk or heavy cream and butter over low heat until the butter is melted. Keep warm.

Mash the Potatoes:
- Using a potato masher or a ricer, mash the potatoes to your desired consistency. Some people prefer smooth mashed potatoes, while others like them a bit chunky.

Add the Milk Mixture:
- Gradually add the warm milk and butter mixture to the mashed potatoes, stirring or mashing continuously. Continue until you achieve the desired creamy texture.

Season:
- Season the mashed potatoes with salt and black pepper to taste. Adjust the seasoning as needed.

Garnish (Optional):
- If desired, garnish the mashed potatoes with chopped fresh chives or parsley.

Serve Warm:
- Serve the creamy mashed potatoes immediately while they are warm.

Tips:

- Variations: Experiment with variations like adding roasted garlic, grated cheese, or sour cream for extra flavor.
- Keep Warm: If you're not serving the mashed potatoes immediately, cover the pot with a lid to keep them warm. You can also reheat them gently on the stove or in the microwave.

These creamy mashed potatoes are a timeless and versatile side dish that complements a wide range of meals. Whether served on Thanksgiving or any other occasion, they are sure to be a crowd-pleaser.

Stuffing/Dressing

Ingredients:

- 1 loaf of day-old bread (white, whole wheat, or a mix), cut into cubes
- 1/2 cup (1 stick) unsalted butter
- 1 large onion, finely chopped
- 2-3 celery stalks, finely chopped
- 2-3 cloves garlic, minced
- 2-3 cups chicken or vegetable broth
- 2 teaspoons dried sage
- 1 teaspoon dried thyme
- 1 teaspoon dried rosemary
- Salt and black pepper to taste
- 2 large eggs, beaten (optional, for added richness)
- Chopped fresh parsley for garnish

Instructions:

Prepare the Bread Cubes:
- Cut the day-old bread into 1-inch cubes. If the bread is not already stale, you can spread the cubes on a baking sheet and let them dry out for a few hours or overnight.

Preheat the Oven:
- Preheat your oven to 350°F (175°C).

Sauté Vegetables:
- In a large skillet, melt the butter over medium heat. Add chopped onions, celery, and garlic. Sauté until the vegetables are softened, about 5-7 minutes.

Add Herbs:
- Stir in the dried sage, thyme, and rosemary. Cook for an additional 2-3 minutes, allowing the herbs to become fragrant.

Combine Bread and Vegetables:
- In a large mixing bowl, combine the bread cubes with the sautéed vegetables and herbs. Toss to mix evenly.

Moisten with Broth:
- Gradually add chicken or vegetable broth to the bread mixture until it is moistened to your liking. Be careful not to make it too soggy; you can always add more broth later if needed.

Season:

- Season the stuffing with salt and black pepper to taste. Adjust the seasoning as needed.

Optional: Add Eggs:
- If you like a richer stuffing, you can beat the eggs and fold them into the mixture at this point.

Bake:
- Transfer the stuffing to a baking dish. Cover with foil and bake in the preheated oven for 30 minutes. Remove the foil and bake for an additional 15-20 minutes or until the top is golden brown.

Garnish and Serve:
- Garnish the stuffing with chopped fresh parsley before serving. Serve warm alongside your Thanksgiving turkey.

Tips:

- Customize: Feel free to add other ingredients like sautéed mushrooms, chopped nuts, or dried fruit for additional flavor and texture.
- Make-Ahead: You can prepare the stuffing up to a day in advance. Keep it refrigerated until ready to bake, and adjust the baking time as needed.

This classic stuffing recipe is a versatile base that you can modify to suit your preferences. Whether baked inside the turkey or separately, it's a comforting and flavorful addition to your Thanksgiving feast.

Sweet Potato Casserole

Ingredients:

For the Sweet Potatoes:

- 4 cups mashed sweet potatoes (about 3-4 large sweet potatoes, cooked and peeled)
- 1/2 cup unsalted butter, melted
- 1/2 cup milk (whole or evaporated)
- 1/2 cup granulated sugar
- 2 large eggs
- 1 teaspoon vanilla extract
- 1/2 teaspoon salt

For the Pecan Streusel Topping:

- 1 cup chopped pecans
- 1/2 cup all-purpose flour
- 1/2 cup brown sugar, packed
- 1/4 cup unsalted butter, melted

Instructions:

Preheat the Oven:
- Preheat your oven to 350°F (175°C).

Cook and Mash Sweet Potatoes:
- Wash and peel the sweet potatoes. Cut them into chunks and boil or steam until tender. Mash the cooked sweet potatoes in a large mixing bowl.

Prepare the Sweet Potato Base:
- To the mashed sweet potatoes, add melted butter, milk, granulated sugar, eggs, vanilla extract, and salt. Mix until well combined.

Transfer to Baking Dish:
- Transfer the sweet potato mixture to a greased baking dish, spreading it evenly.

Prepare the Streusel Topping:
- In a separate bowl, mix together chopped pecans, flour, brown sugar, and melted butter to create the streusel topping.

Add Streusel Topping:
- Sprinkle the pecan streusel topping evenly over the sweet potato mixture in the baking dish.

- Bake:
  - Bake in the preheated oven for 25-30 minutes or until the top is golden brown and the casserole is heated through.
- Serve Warm:
  - Allow the Sweet Potato Casserole to cool slightly before serving. It can be served warm as a side dish.

Tips:

- Marshmallow Topping: If you prefer a marshmallow topping, you can add a layer of marshmallows on top during the last 5-10 minutes of baking until they are golden brown.

This Sweet Potato Casserole with pecan streusel is a delightful blend of sweet and nutty flavors, making it a perfect addition to your Thanksgiving table. It's a crowd-pleaser that will have everyone coming back for seconds.

Green Bean Casserole

Ingredients:

For the Casserole:

- 1 1/2 pounds fresh green beans, trimmed and cut into bite-sized pieces
- 1 can (10.5 ounces) cream of mushroom soup
- 1/2 cup milk
- 1 teaspoon soy sauce
- 1/2 teaspoon black pepper
- 1 cup crispy fried onions (French's Fried Onions or homemade)

For the Topping:

- 1 cup crispy fried onions

Instructions:

Preheat the Oven:
- Preheat your oven to 350°F (175°C).

Blanch the Green Beans:
- Bring a large pot of water to a boil. Add salt and the trimmed green beans. Blanch the green beans for about 3-4 minutes until they are bright green and slightly tender. Drain and immediately transfer to an ice bath to stop the cooking process. Drain again.

Prepare the Casserole Mixture:
- In a mixing bowl, combine cream of mushroom soup, milk, soy sauce, and black pepper. Stir until well mixed.

Combine with Green Beans:
- Add the blanched green beans to the bowl and toss until the green beans are well coated with the soup mixture.

Add Crispy Fried Onions:
- Stir in 1 cup of crispy fried onions into the green bean mixture.

Transfer to Baking Dish:
- Transfer the green bean mixture to a greased baking dish, spreading it out evenly.

Top with Remaining Crispy Fried Onions:
- Sprinkle the remaining crispy fried onions evenly over the top of the green bean mixture.

Bake:
- Bake in the preheated oven for 25-30 minutes or until the casserole is hot and bubbly, and the crispy fried onions on top are golden brown.

Serve Warm:
- Allow the Green Bean Casserole to cool slightly before serving. It's best served warm.

Tips:

- Homemade Fried Onions: You can make your own crispy fried onions by thinly slicing onions, coating them in flour, and frying until golden brown.

This classic Green Bean Casserole is a crowd-pleaser and a great addition to your Thanksgiving or holiday dinner menu. Its creamy texture and crispy fried onion topping make it a comforting and flavorful side dish.

Brussels Sprouts with Bacon

Ingredients:

- 1 pound Brussels sprouts, trimmed and halved
- 6 slices bacon, chopped
- 1 tablespoon olive oil
- 2 cloves garlic, minced
- Salt and black pepper to taste
- Optional: Grated Parmesan cheese for garnish

Instructions:

Preheat the Oven:
- Preheat your oven to 400°F (200°C).

Prepare Brussels Sprouts:
- Trim the Brussels sprouts and cut them in half.

Cook Bacon:
- In a large oven-safe skillet, cook the chopped bacon over medium heat until it becomes crispy. Use a slotted spoon to transfer the cooked bacon to a plate lined with paper towels.

Sauté Brussels Sprouts:
- In the same skillet with the bacon fat, add olive oil. Add the halved Brussels sprouts and sauté them for about 5 minutes, or until they start to brown.

Add Garlic:
- Add minced garlic to the Brussels sprouts and cook for an additional 1-2 minutes until the garlic becomes fragrant.

Combine with Bacon:
- Mix the cooked bacon back into the Brussels sprouts, combining the flavors.

Season:
- Season the Brussels sprouts with salt and black pepper to taste. Keep in mind that the bacon adds saltiness, so adjust accordingly.

Roast in the Oven:
- Transfer the skillet to the preheated oven and roast for about 15-20 minutes or until the Brussels sprouts are tender and have crispy edges.

Optional: Add Parmesan Cheese:
- If desired, sprinkle grated Parmesan cheese over the Brussels sprouts during the last 5 minutes of roasting.

Serve Warm:
- Remove the skillet from the oven and serve the Brussels Sprouts with Bacon warm.

Tips:

- Variations: Add a drizzle of balsamic glaze or a squeeze of lemon juice for extra flavor.
- Crispy Texture: For extra crispiness, you can broil the Brussels sprouts for the last 1-2 minutes of roasting.

Brussels Sprouts with Bacon is a delightful and savory side dish that pairs well with various main courses. The combination of crispy bacon and roasted Brussels sprouts creates a perfect balance of flavors.

Gravy:

Turkey Gravy

Ingredients:

- Drippings from a roasted turkey
- 1/4 cup all-purpose flour
- 4 cups turkey or chicken broth (homemade or store-bought)
- Salt and black pepper to taste
- Optional: Giblets (turkey neck, heart, and gizzard), finely chopped
- Optional: 1/4 cup dry white wine or turkey/chicken drippings
- Optional: Fresh herbs (thyme, sage, rosemary)

Instructions:

Collect Drippings:
- After roasting your turkey, collect the drippings from the roasting pan. Pour the drippings through a fine-mesh strainer into a bowl to remove any solid bits. Set aside.

Prepare Broth:
- In a saucepan, heat turkey or chicken broth over medium heat. If you have giblets, you can also simmer them in the broth to enhance flavor. Add fresh herbs if desired.

Make Roux:
- In a separate pan, melt 1/4 cup of the turkey fat or butter over medium heat. Add flour and whisk continuously to form a roux. Cook the roux for 2-3 minutes until it turns golden brown.

Combine Roux and Broth:
- Slowly pour the hot broth into the roux, whisking continuously to avoid lumps. Continue whisking until the gravy thickens. If needed, use a strainer to catch any lumps.

Add Drippings:
- Pour in the reserved turkey drippings, continuing to whisk the gravy. This adds depth of flavor.

Season:
- Season the gravy with salt and black pepper to taste. If you like, you can also add a splash of dry white wine or more turkey/chicken drippings for additional flavor.

Simmer:

- Allow the gravy to simmer over low heat for 10-15 minutes, stirring occasionally. This helps the flavors meld and the gravy to thicken.

Adjust Consistency:
- If the gravy is too thick, you can add more broth. If it's too thin, let it simmer a bit longer or mix a small amount of flour with cold water and whisk it into the gravy.

Strain (Optional):
- For a smoother texture, you can strain the gravy through a fine-mesh strainer before serving.

Serve Warm:
- Once the gravy reaches your desired consistency and flavor, remove it from heat and serve it warm alongside your turkey and other Thanksgiving dishes.

Tips:

- Customize: Feel free to customize your gravy by adding herbs, a dash of Worcestershire sauce, or a splash of balsamic vinegar for additional depth of flavor.
- Make-Ahead: You can make the gravy ahead of time and reheat it just before serving. If it thickens upon reheating, adjust the consistency with a bit of broth.

This homemade turkey gravy is a wonderful complement to your Thanksgiving turkey, mashed potatoes, and stuffing, bringing all the flavors together into a delicious and comforting dish.

Cranberry Sauce:

Homemade Cranberry Sauce

Ingredients:

- 1 bag (12 ounces) fresh or frozen cranberries
- 1 cup granulated sugar
- 1 cup water
- Zest of one orange (optional)
- 1-2 tablespoons fresh orange juice (optional)

Instructions:

Rinse Cranberries:
- Rinse the cranberries thoroughly under cold water and remove any stems or blemished berries.

Combine Ingredients:
- In a medium saucepan, combine the cranberries, sugar, and water.

Add Orange Zest and Juice (Optional):
- If desired, add the zest of one orange for extra flavor. You can also add 1-2 tablespoons of fresh orange juice to enhance the citrus notes.

Bring to a Boil:
- Bring the mixture to a boil over medium-high heat. Stir occasionally to dissolve the sugar.

Simmer:
- Reduce the heat to medium-low and let the mixture simmer for about 10-15 minutes or until the cranberries burst and the sauce thickens.

Adjust Sweetness:
- Taste the cranberry sauce and adjust the sweetness if needed by adding more sugar.

Cool:
- Remove the saucepan from heat and allow the cranberry sauce to cool. It will continue to thicken as it cools.

Serve or Refrigerate:
- Once cooled, transfer the cranberry sauce to a serving dish. You can serve it immediately, or cover and refrigerate for at least a few hours or overnight.

Garnish (Optional):

- If desired, garnish with a few whole cranberries or a twist of orange zest before serving.

Tips:

- Texture Preference: If you prefer a smoother sauce, you can use a potato masher or blend the cranberry sauce with an immersion blender after cooking.
- Make-Ahead: Cranberry sauce can be made a day or two in advance and stored in the refrigerator until serving.

Homemade cranberry sauce is a delightful addition to your Thanksgiving table, providing a burst of tartness and vibrant color. Enjoy making and savoring this classic holiday condiment!

Breads:

Classic Dinner Rolls

Ingredients:

- 4 to 4 1/2 cups all-purpose flour
- 1/4 cup granulated sugar
- 1 tablespoon active dry yeast
- 1 teaspoon salt
- 1 cup warm milk (about 110°F or 43°C)
- 1/4 cup unsalted butter, melted
- 1 large egg

Instructions:

- Activate Yeast:
    - In a small bowl, combine warm milk and a pinch of sugar. Sprinkle the active dry yeast over the warm milk and let it sit for 5-10 minutes until it becomes frothy.
- Mix Dry Ingredients:
    - In a large mixing bowl, whisk together 4 cups of all-purpose flour, sugar, and salt.
- Combine Wet Ingredients:
    - Make a well in the center of the dry ingredients. Pour in the activated yeast mixture, melted butter, and beaten egg.
- Knead Dough:
    - Mix the wet and dry ingredients until a soft dough forms. Turn the dough out onto a floured surface and knead for about 8-10 minutes until it becomes smooth and elastic. Add more flour if the dough is too sticky.
- First Rise:
    - Place the dough in a greased bowl, cover it with a clean kitchen towel, and let it rise in a warm place for about 1-1.5 hours or until it doubles in size.
- Shape Rolls:
    - Punch down the risen dough and turn it out onto a floured surface. Divide the dough into 12-15 equal portions. Shape each portion into a round ball and place them in a greased baking dish, leaving a little space between each roll.
- Second Rise:

- Cover the baking dish with a towel and let the rolls rise for another 30-45 minutes.

Preheat Oven:
- Preheat your oven to 375°F (190°C).

Bake:
- Bake the rolls in the preheated oven for 15-20 minutes or until they are golden brown on top.

Brush with Butter (Optional):
- If desired, brush the warm rolls with melted butter for a shiny finish.

Cool and Serve:
- Allow the dinner rolls to cool slightly before serving. Serve them warm with butter.

Tips:

- Make-Ahead: You can make the dough ahead of time, refrigerate it after the first rise, and shape the rolls just before baking.
- Freezing: Dinner rolls can be frozen after baking. Thaw and reheat in a warm oven before serving.

These classic dinner rolls are soft, fluffy, and perfect for any holiday meal. Enjoy the aroma of freshly baked rolls wafting through your kitchen!

Cornbread

Ingredients:

- 1 cup yellow cornmeal
- 1 cup all-purpose flour
- 1 tablespoon baking powder
- 1/2 teaspoon baking soda
- 1/2 teaspoon salt
- 2 tablespoons granulated sugar (optional, for a slightly sweet cornbread)
- 1 cup buttermilk
- 2 large eggs
- 1/2 cup unsalted butter, melted

Instructions:

Preheat the Oven:
- Preheat your oven to 400°F (200°C). Grease a 9-inch square baking pan or a similar-sized cast-iron skillet.

Mix Dry Ingredients:
- In a large mixing bowl, whisk together the cornmeal, flour, baking powder, baking soda, salt, and sugar (if using).

Combine Wet Ingredients:
- In a separate bowl, whisk together the buttermilk, eggs, and melted butter.

Combine Wet and Dry Ingredients:
- Pour the wet ingredients into the dry ingredients and stir until just combined. Be careful not to overmix; a few lumps are okay.

Pour into Baking Pan:
- Pour the batter into the prepared baking pan or skillet, spreading it evenly.

Bake:
- Bake in the preheated oven for 20-25 minutes, or until the top is golden brown and a toothpick inserted into the center comes out clean.

Cool and Serve:
- Allow the cornbread to cool in the pan for a few minutes before slicing and serving. Serve it warm with butter or your favorite topping.

Tips:

- Customize: Feel free to add extras like chopped jalapeños, grated cheese, or corn kernels for added flavor and texture.

- Buttermilk Substitute: If you don't have buttermilk, you can make a substitute by adding 1 tablespoon of vinegar or lemon juice to a cup of milk and letting it sit for 5 minutes.

This homemade cornbread recipe produces a moist and slightly crumbly bread with a golden crust. It's perfect for serving alongside chili, soups, stews, or as a side dish for your Thanksgiving feast. Enjoy!

Soups:

Butternut Squash Soup

Ingredients:

- 1 large butternut squash, peeled, seeded, and cubed (about 4 cups)
- 1 large carrot, peeled and chopped
- 1 onion, chopped
- 2 cloves garlic, minced
- 2 tablespoons olive oil
- 4 cups vegetable or chicken broth
- 1 teaspoon ground cumin
- 1/2 teaspoon ground cinnamon
- 1/4 teaspoon ground nutmeg
- Salt and black pepper to taste
- 1/2 cup heavy cream (optional, for added creaminess)
- Chopped fresh parsley or chives for garnish

Instructions:

Preheat the Oven:
- Preheat your oven to 400°F (200°C).

Roast the Vegetables:
- In a large baking sheet, toss the butternut squash, carrot, onion, and minced garlic with olive oil. Spread them out in a single layer. Roast in the preheated oven for about 30-40 minutes or until the vegetables are tender and slightly caramelized.

Blend Vegetables:
- Transfer the roasted vegetables to a blender or food processor. Add a cup of broth and blend until smooth. You may need to do this in batches.

Cook in Pot:
- Pour the blended mixture into a large pot. Add the remaining broth, ground cumin, cinnamon, nutmeg, salt, and black pepper. Stir well.

Simmer:
- Bring the soup to a simmer over medium heat. Let it simmer for about 10-15 minutes, allowing the flavors to meld.

Adjust Seasoning:

- Taste the soup and adjust the seasoning if needed. You can add more salt, pepper, or spices according to your preference.

Add Cream (Optional):
- If using heavy cream, stir it into the soup for added creaminess. Simmer for an additional 5 minutes.

Serve:
- Ladle the butternut squash soup into bowls. Garnish with chopped fresh parsley or chives.

Tips:

- Garnish Ideas: Try topping the soup with a drizzle of olive oil, a dollop of sour cream, or a sprinkle of toasted pumpkin seeds.
- Make-Ahead: This soup can be made ahead of time and reheated before serving. The flavors often deepen after sitting for a day.

This butternut squash soup is both comforting and nutritious, making it a perfect starter or side for your Thanksgiving or fall meals. Enjoy the warm and rich flavors!

Roasted Pumpkin Soup

Ingredients:

- 1 small to medium-sized pumpkin (about 4 cups of pumpkin puree)
- 1 onion, chopped
- 2 cloves garlic, minced
- 2 tablespoons olive oil
- 4 cups vegetable or chicken broth
- 1 teaspoon ground cumin
- 1/2 teaspoon ground cinnamon
- 1/4 teaspoon ground nutmeg
- Salt and black pepper to taste
- 1/2 cup heavy cream (optional, for added creaminess)
- Roasted pumpkin seeds for garnish
- Chopped fresh parsley or chives for garnish

Instructions:

Preheat the Oven:
- Preheat your oven to 400°F (200°C).

Prepare the Pumpkin:
- Cut the pumpkin in half, scoop out the seeds (save them for roasting if you like), and place the pumpkin halves on a baking sheet, cut side up.

Roast the Pumpkin:
- Drizzle the pumpkin halves with olive oil and sprinkle with salt. Roast in the preheated oven for about 45-60 minutes or until the pumpkin flesh is fork-tender. Remove from the oven and let it cool slightly.

Scoop and Puree:
- Scoop out the roasted pumpkin flesh and transfer it to a blender or food processor. Blend until you have a smooth puree. You can also use an immersion blender directly in the roasting pan.

Sauté Onion and Garlic:
- In a large pot, heat olive oil over medium heat. Add chopped onion and minced garlic. Sauté until the onion becomes translucent.

Add Pumpkin Puree:
- Pour in the pumpkin puree and stir it into the sautéed onions and garlic.

Add Spices and Broth:
- Add ground cumin, cinnamon, nutmeg, salt, and black pepper to the pot. Pour in the vegetable or chicken broth. Stir well.

Simmer:
- Bring the soup to a simmer and let it cook for about 15-20 minutes, allowing the flavors to meld.

Adjust Seasoning:
- Taste the soup and adjust the seasoning if needed. You can add more salt, pepper, or spices according to your preference.

Add Cream (Optional):
- If using heavy cream, stir it into the soup for added creaminess. Simmer for an additional 5 minutes.

Serve:
- Ladle the roasted pumpkin soup into bowls. Garnish with a drizzle of cream, roasted pumpkin seeds, and chopped fresh parsley or chives.

Tips:

- Customize: Experiment with additional spices like ginger or curry powder for different flavor profiles.
- Texture Preference: If you prefer a chunkier soup, you can leave some small pieces of roasted pumpkin in the mix.

This roasted pumpkin soup is a delightful and comforting dish that captures the essence of fall. Enjoy the rich and earthy flavors!

Salads:

Harvest Salad

Ingredients:

For the Salad:

- 6 cups mixed salad greens (such as arugula, spinach, and/or mixed lettuces)
- 1 cup roasted butternut squash, diced
- 1 cup apple slices (use a crisp variety like Honeycrisp or Gala)
- 1/2 cup dried cranberries
- 1/2 cup pecans, toasted
- 1/4 cup crumbled feta or goat cheese
- Seeds of 1 pomegranate (optional)
- Salt and black pepper to taste

For the Maple Balsamic Vinaigrette:

- 1/4 cup balsamic vinegar
- 1/4 cup extra-virgin olive oil
- 2 tablespoons maple syrup
- 1 teaspoon Dijon mustard
- Salt and black pepper to taste

Instructions:

Prepare Salad Ingredients:
- In a large salad bowl, combine the mixed greens, roasted butternut squash, apple slices, dried cranberries, toasted pecans, and crumbled feta or goat cheese.

Prepare Vinaigrette:
- In a small bowl or jar, whisk together balsamic vinegar, olive oil, maple syrup, Dijon mustard, salt, and black pepper. Adjust the sweetness and acidity to your liking.

Toss the Salad:
- Drizzle the maple balsamic vinaigrette over the salad ingredients. Gently toss the salad to coat all the ingredients evenly.

Season:
- Season the salad with salt and black pepper to taste.

Garnish with Pomegranate Seeds (Optional):

- If using, sprinkle pomegranate seeds over the top for added color and flavor.

Serve:
- Divide the Harvest Salad among plates or serve it in a large bowl. Optionally, you can add additional toppings like grilled chicken or roasted turkey for a heartier version.

Tips:

- Make-Ahead: You can prepare the salad ingredients and dressing ahead of time, keeping them separate until ready to serve.
- Customize: Feel free to add other seasonal ingredients like sliced pear, roasted sweet potatoes, or candied nuts.

This Harvest Salad with maple balsamic vinaigrette is a delightful combination of sweet, savory, and tangy flavors, making it a perfect addition to your fall or Thanksgiving menu.

Enjoy the abundance of seasonal ingredients!

Cranberry Walnut Salad

Ingredients:

For the Salad:

- 6 cups mixed salad greens (spring mix or your favorite blend)
- 1 cup dried cranberries
- 1 cup chopped walnuts, toasted
- 1/2 cup crumbled feta or goat cheese
- 1 medium apple, thinly sliced
- 1/4 red onion, thinly sliced

For the Honey Mustard Vinaigrette:

- 1/4 cup extra-virgin olive oil
- 2 tablespoons balsamic vinegar
- 1 tablespoon Dijon mustard
- 1 tablespoon honey
- Salt and black pepper to taste

Instructions:

Prepare Salad Ingredients:
- In a large salad bowl, combine the mixed salad greens, dried cranberries, toasted walnuts, crumbled feta or goat cheese, sliced apple, and thinly sliced red onion.

Prepare Vinaigrette:
- In a small bowl or jar, whisk together the extra-virgin olive oil, balsamic vinegar, Dijon mustard, honey, salt, and black pepper. Adjust the sweetness and acidity to your liking.

Toss the Salad:
- Drizzle the honey mustard vinaigrette over the salad ingredients. Gently toss the salad to coat all the ingredients evenly.

Season:
- Season the salad with additional salt and black pepper if needed.

Serve:
- Divide the Cranberry Walnut Salad among plates or serve it in a large bowl.

Tips:

- Toasting Walnuts: Toast the walnuts in a dry skillet over medium heat for a few minutes until they become fragrant. Be sure to watch them closely to prevent burning.

This Cranberry Walnut Salad is a delightful combination of sweet, tangy, and nutty flavors. It's a perfect addition to your holiday table or a light and refreshing side for any occasion. Enjoy!

Potatoes:

Scalloped Potatoes

Ingredients:

- 2 pounds russet potatoes, peeled and thinly sliced
- 1/4 cup unsalted butter
- 1/4 cup all-purpose flour
- 2 cups whole milk
- 1 cup heavy cream
- 2 cloves garlic, minced
- 1 teaspoon salt
- 1/2 teaspoon black pepper
- 2 cups shredded sharp cheddar cheese
- 1/2 cup grated Parmesan cheese
- Fresh thyme or chopped parsley for garnish (optional)

Instructions:

Preheat the Oven:
- Preheat your oven to 350°F (175°C). Grease a 9x13-inch baking dish.

Slice Potatoes:
- Peel and thinly slice the potatoes, aiming for slices of uniform thickness.

Prepare Cheese Sauce:
- In a medium saucepan over medium heat, melt the butter. Add the minced garlic and cook for about 1 minute until fragrant. Stir in the flour to create a roux.

Make Roux:
- Cook the roux for 1-2 minutes, stirring constantly. Gradually whisk in the milk and heavy cream to avoid lumps. Continue cooking and stirring until the mixture thickens.

Season:
- Add salt and black pepper to the sauce, adjusting to taste.

Add Cheese:
- Reduce the heat to low and stir in the shredded cheddar cheese until melted and smooth.

Layer Potatoes:

- Arrange a layer of sliced potatoes in the prepared baking dish. Pour a portion of the cheese sauce over the potatoes, spreading it evenly. Repeat the layers until all the potatoes and sauce are used, finishing with a layer of cheese sauce on top.

Sprinkle Parmesan:
- Sprinkle grated Parmesan cheese over the top for an extra cheesy crust.

Bake:
- Cover the baking dish with foil and bake in the preheated oven for about 45 minutes. Then, uncover and bake for an additional 15-20 minutes or until the top is golden brown and the potatoes are tender when pierced with a fork.

Rest and Garnish:
- Allow the scalloped potatoes to rest for a few minutes before serving. Optionally, garnish with fresh thyme or chopped parsley.

Tips:

- Even Slicing: For uniform cooking, try to slice the potatoes evenly. You can use a mandoline slicer for precision.
- Make-Ahead: You can assemble the dish ahead of time and refrigerate it. Bake when ready to serve.

These creamy and cheesy scalloped potatoes are a crowd-pleaser and make a wonderful side dish for any holiday or special meal. Enjoy the rich and comforting flavors!

Garlic Mashed Potatoes

Ingredients:

- 2 1/2 pounds russet potatoes, peeled and cut into chunks
- 4 cloves garlic, peeled and minced
- 1/2 cup unsalted butter
- 1 cup whole milk or heavy cream
- Salt and black pepper to taste
- Chopped fresh chives or parsley for garnish (optional)

Instructions:

Boil Potatoes:
- Place the peeled and chopped potatoes in a large pot of salted water. Bring to a boil and cook until the potatoes are fork-tender, about 15-20 minutes.

Prepare Garlic Butter:
- While the potatoes are boiling, melt the butter in a small saucepan over medium heat. Add the minced garlic and cook for 1-2 minutes until fragrant. Be careful not to let the garlic brown.

Drain Potatoes:
- Drain the cooked potatoes and return them to the pot.

Mash Potatoes:
- Mash the potatoes using a potato masher or a ricer until they are smooth and free of lumps.

Add Garlic Butter:
- Pour the garlic-infused butter over the mashed potatoes.

Heat Milk or Cream:
- In a separate saucepan, heat the milk or heavy cream until warm but not boiling.

Add Warm Milk or Cream:
- Gradually add the warm milk or cream to the mashed potatoes, stirring continuously. Add it in small amounts until you achieve your desired creamy consistency.

Season:
- Season the mashed potatoes with salt and black pepper to taste. Adjust the seasoning as needed.

Garnish:

- Optionally, garnish with chopped fresh chives or parsley for a pop of color and added flavor.

Serve Warm:
- Serve the garlic mashed potatoes warm as a delicious side dish.

Tips:

- Roasted Garlic Variation: For a deeper and slightly sweet garlic flavor, you can roast the garlic cloves in the oven before adding them to the butter.
- Make-Ahead: You can make these mashed potatoes a day ahead and reheat them on the stovetop or in the microwave.

These garlic mashed potatoes are creamy, flavorful, and the perfect complement to your holiday feast or any family dinner. Enjoy!

Vegetarian Options:

Stuffed Acorn Squash

Ingredients:

For the Stuffed Acorn Squash:

- 3 acorn squash, halved and seeds removed
- 2 tablespoons olive oil
- Salt and black pepper to taste
- 1 cup quinoa, rinsed and cooked according to package instructions
- 1 can (15 oz) black beans, drained and rinsed
- 1 cup corn kernels (fresh or frozen)
- 1 cup cherry tomatoes, halved
- 1 cup red bell pepper, diced
- 1 cup spinach or kale, chopped
- 1/2 cup feta or goat cheese, crumbled (optional)
- 1 teaspoon cumin
- 1 teaspoon chili powder
- 1/2 teaspoon smoked paprika
- 1/4 teaspoon cayenne pepper (optional for extra heat)
- Fresh cilantro or parsley for garnish

For the Avocado Crema:

- 2 ripe avocados
- 1/4 cup Greek yogurt or sour cream
- 1 clove garlic, minced
- 2 tablespoons lime juice
- Salt and black pepper to taste

Instructions:

Preheat the Oven:
- Preheat your oven to 400°F (200°C).

Prepare Acorn Squash:
- Brush the cut sides of the acorn squash halves with olive oil and season with salt and black pepper. Place them on a baking sheet, cut side down. Roast in the preheated oven for about 30-40 minutes or until the squash is tender.

Prepare Quinoa:
- While the squash is roasting, cook the quinoa according to package instructions.

Prepare Filling:
- In a large bowl, combine the cooked quinoa, black beans, corn, cherry tomatoes, red bell pepper, chopped spinach or kale, cumin, chili powder, smoked paprika, and cayenne pepper. Mix well.

Stuff the Squash:
- Once the squash is tender, flip them over, and fill each cavity with the quinoa and vegetable mixture. If using, sprinkle crumbled feta or goat cheese on top.

Bake:
- Return the stuffed squash to the oven and bake for an additional 10-15 minutes, or until the filling is heated through.

Prepare Avocado Crema:
- In a blender or food processor, combine ripe avocados, Greek yogurt or sour cream, minced garlic, lime juice, salt, and black pepper. Blend until smooth.

Serve:
- Remove the stuffed acorn squash from the oven. Drizzle with avocado crema and garnish with fresh cilantro or parsley.

Tips:

- Variations: Feel free to customize the filling with your favorite vegetables, nuts, or herbs.
- Protein Boost: Add cooked chickpeas, tofu, or your favorite plant-based protein to make the dish more substantial.

This Vegetarian Stuffed Acorn Squash is not only visually appealing but also packed with flavorful and nutritious ingredients. It's a perfect option for a festive and satisfying vegetarian meal. Enjoy!

Vegetarian Wellington

Ingredients:

For the Mushroom Duxelles:

- 1 pound cremini or button mushrooms, finely chopped
- 2 shallots, finely chopped
- 2 cloves garlic, minced
- 2 tablespoons olive oil
- Salt and black pepper to taste
- 2 tablespoons fresh thyme, chopped

For the Spinach and Cheese Filling:

- 1 pound fresh spinach, washed and chopped
- 1 cup ricotta cheese
- 1 cup grated Parmesan cheese
- 1/2 cup breadcrumbs
- 2 cloves garlic, minced
- Salt and black pepper to taste
- 1/4 teaspoon nutmeg (optional)

For Assembly:

- 1 sheet puff pastry, thawed if frozen
- 1 egg, beaten (for egg wash)

Instructions:

Mushroom Duxelles:

    Sauté Mushrooms:
- In a large pan, heat olive oil over medium heat. Add chopped mushrooms, shallots, and garlic. Cook, stirring occasionally, until the mushrooms release their moisture and become golden brown.

    Season:
- Season with salt, black pepper, and fresh thyme. Continue cooking until most of the moisture has evaporated. Remove from heat and let it cool.

Spinach and Cheese Filling:

Cook Spinach:
- In the same pan, add chopped spinach and cook until wilted. Drain any excess liquid.

Prepare Filling:
- In a bowl, combine cooked spinach, ricotta cheese, Parmesan cheese, breadcrumbs, minced garlic, salt, black pepper, and nutmeg. Mix well.

Assembly:

Preheat Oven:
- Preheat your oven to 400°F (200°C).

Roll Out Puff Pastry:
- On a lightly floured surface, roll out the puff pastry into a rectangle large enough to encase the filling.

Spread Mushroom Duxelles:
- Spread the mushroom duxelles over the puff pastry, leaving a border around the edges.

Layer Spinach and Cheese Filling:
- Place the spinach and cheese filling over the mushroom layer.

Roll and Seal:
- Carefully roll the puff pastry over the filling, creating a log shape. Seal the edges by pinching them together.

Brush with Egg Wash:
- Place the Wellington seam side down on a baking sheet. Brush the surface with beaten egg for a golden finish.

Bake:
- Bake in the preheated oven for 25-30 minutes or until the puff pastry is golden brown and crispy.

Rest and Serve:
- Allow the Vegetarian Wellington to rest for a few minutes before slicing. Serve with your favorite vegetarian gravy or sauce.

Tips:

- Puff Pastry Handling: Work quickly with the puff pastry to prevent it from becoming too warm. If needed, refrigerate it for a few minutes during the assembly process.
- Make-Ahead: You can prepare the mushroom duxelles and spinach filling ahead of time, and assemble the Wellington just before baking.

This Vegetarian Wellington is a flavorful and satisfying alternative for those looking for a meatless option. It's sure to impress your guests with its layers of rich and savory goodness. Enjoy!

Desserts - Pies:

Pumpkin Pie

Ingredients:

For the Pie Crust:

- 1 1/4 cups all-purpose flour
- 1/2 cup unsalted butter, chilled and cubed
- 1/4 cup granulated sugar
- 1/4 teaspoon salt
- 2-3 tablespoons ice water

For the Pumpkin Filling:

- 1 can (15 ounces) pure pumpkin puree
- 3/4 cup granulated sugar
- 1 teaspoon ground cinnamon
- 1/2 teaspoon ground ginger
- 1/4 teaspoon ground cloves
- 1/2 teaspoon salt
- 2 large eggs
- 1 can (12 ounces) evaporated milk

Optional for Serving:

- Whipped cream
- Ground cinnamon or nutmeg for garnish

Instructions:

Pie Crust:

    Prepare the Dough:
- In a food processor, combine the flour, sugar, and salt. Add the chilled butter cubes and pulse until the mixture resembles coarse crumbs.

    Add Ice Water:
- Gradually add ice water, one tablespoon at a time, and pulse until the dough just comes together. Be careful not to overmix.

    Form a Disk:

- Turn the dough out onto a lightly floured surface and gather it into a disk. Wrap in plastic wrap and refrigerate for at least 30 minutes.

Roll Out the Crust:
- Preheat your oven to 375°F (190°C). On a floured surface, roll out the chilled dough into a 12-inch circle. Transfer the crust to a 9-inch pie dish, trim the excess, and crimp the edges.

Pumpkin Filling:

Preheat Oven:
- Preheat your oven to 425°F (220°C).

Mix Pumpkin Filling:
- In a large bowl, whisk together pumpkin puree, sugar, cinnamon, ginger, cloves, and salt. Add eggs and whisk until well combined. Gradually add the evaporated milk, mixing until smooth.

Fill the Pie Shell:
- Pour the pumpkin filling into the prepared pie crust.

Bake:
- Bake in the preheated oven for 15 minutes. Reduce the oven temperature to 350°F (175°C) and continue baking for an additional 40-50 minutes, or until a knife inserted near the center comes out clean.

Cool:
- Allow the pumpkin pie to cool completely on a wire rack.

Chill (Optional):
- For best results, refrigerate the pumpkin pie for a few hours or overnight before serving.

Serve:
- Serve slices of pumpkin pie with a dollop of whipped cream and a sprinkle of ground cinnamon or nutmeg.

Tips:

- Blind Baking: If you prefer a crispier crust, you can blind-bake the crust before adding the filling. To do this, line the crust with parchment paper and fill it with pie weights or dried beans before baking for about 15 minutes, then remove the weights and continue baking.

Enjoy the warm, spiced goodness of homemade pumpkin pie – a classic treat that's perfect for autumn celebrations!

Pecan Pie

Ingredients:

For the Pie Crust (or you can use a store-bought crust):

- 1 1/4 cups all-purpose flour
- 1/2 cup unsalted butter, chilled and cubed
- 1/4 teaspoon salt
- 2-3 tablespoons ice water

For the Pecan Filling:

- 1 cup granulated sugar
- 1 cup light corn syrup
- 1/2 cup unsalted butter, melted
- 1 teaspoon vanilla extract
- 1/4 teaspoon salt
- 3 large eggs
- 2 cups pecan halves

Instructions:

Pie Crust:

    Prepare the Dough:
- In a food processor, combine the flour and salt. Add the chilled butter cubes and pulse until the mixture resembles coarse crumbs.

    Add Ice Water:
- Gradually add ice water, one tablespoon at a time, and pulse until the dough just comes together. Be careful not to overmix.

    Form a Disk:
- Turn the dough out onto a lightly floured surface and gather it into a disk. Wrap in plastic wrap and refrigerate for at least 30 minutes.

    Roll Out the Crust:
- Preheat your oven to 375°F (190°C). On a floured surface, roll out the chilled dough into a 12-inch circle. Transfer the crust to a 9-inch pie dish, trim the excess, and crimp the edges.

Pecan Filling:

    Preheat Oven:

- Preheat your oven to 350°F (175°C).

Mix Pecan Filling:
- In a large bowl, whisk together sugar, corn syrup, melted butter, vanilla extract, and salt until well combined. Add eggs and whisk until the mixture is smooth.

Add Pecans:
- Stir in the pecan halves, making sure they are evenly coated with the filling.

Fill the Pie Shell:
- Pour the pecan filling into the prepared pie crust.

Bake:
- Bake in the preheated oven for 50-60 minutes or until the center is set. You can cover the edges of the pie crust with foil if they brown too quickly.

Cool:
- Allow the pecan pie to cool completely on a wire rack before slicing.

Serve:
- Serve slices of pecan pie on its own or with a dollop of whipped cream or a scoop of vanilla ice cream.

Tips:

- Toasting Pecans: For added flavor, you can toast the pecans in a dry skillet over medium heat for a few minutes until they become fragrant before adding them to the filling.
- Make-Ahead: Pecan pie can be made a day in advance and stored at room temperature.

Enjoy this classic pecan pie with its gooey, nutty goodness – a perfect treat for holidays or any special occasion!

Apple Pie

Ingredients:

For the Pie Crust (or you can use a store-bought crust):

- 2 1/2 cups all-purpose flour
- 1 cup unsalted butter, chilled and cubed
- 1 teaspoon salt
- 1 teaspoon granulated sugar
- 1/4 to 1/2 cup ice water

For the Apple Filling:

- 6-7 cups apples (a mix of tart and sweet varieties), peeled, cored, and sliced
- 1/2 to 3/4 cup granulated sugar (adjust based on the sweetness of the apples)
- 1/4 cup brown sugar, packed
- 1 tablespoon lemon juice
- 1 teaspoon ground cinnamon
- 1/4 teaspoon ground nutmeg
- 1/4 teaspoon salt
- 3 tablespoons cornstarch or all-purpose flour

Optional for Serving:

- Vanilla ice cream or whipped cream

Instructions:

Pie Crust:

    Prepare the Dough:
- In a food processor, combine the flour, salt, and sugar. Add the chilled butter cubes and pulse until the mixture resembles coarse crumbs.

    Add Ice Water:
- Gradually add ice water, one tablespoon at a time, and pulse until the dough just comes together. Be careful not to overmix.

    Form Discs:
- Divide the dough into two equal portions, shape each into a disk, wrap in plastic wrap, and refrigerate for at least 1 hour.

    Roll Out the Crust:

- On a floured surface, roll out one disk of dough to fit a 9-inch pie dish. Transfer the crust to the pie dish, trim the excess, and refrigerate while you prepare the filling.

Apple Filling:

Preheat Oven:
- Preheat your oven to 425°F (220°C).

Prepare Apples:
- In a large bowl, toss the sliced apples with lemon juice to prevent browning.

Mix Filling:
- In a separate bowl, combine granulated sugar, brown sugar, cinnamon, nutmeg, salt, and cornstarch or flour. Add this mixture to the sliced apples and toss until the apples are evenly coated.

Fill the Pie Shell:
- Pour the apple filling into the prepared pie crust.

Roll Out Top Crust:
- Roll out the second disk of dough and place it over the apple filling. Trim the excess and crimp the edges to seal the pie.

Ventilation:
- Cut a few slits in the top crust to allow steam to escape during baking.

Bake:
- Bake in the preheated oven for 45-55 minutes or until the crust is golden brown and the filling is bubbly.

Cool:
- Allow the apple pie to cool on a wire rack for at least 2 hours before slicing.

Serve:
- Serve slices of apple pie on its own or with a scoop of vanilla ice cream or a dollop of whipped cream.

Tips:

- Apple Varieties: Use a mix of apples like Granny Smith, Honeycrisp, and Fuji for a balanced flavor and texture.
- Make-Ahead: You can prepare the pie crust and filling in advance and assemble the pie just before baking.

Enjoy the warmth and comforting flavors of homemade apple pie – a timeless dessert that's perfect for any occasion!

Desserts - Other:

Pumpkin Cheesecake

Ingredients:

For the Crust:

- 2 cups graham cracker crumbs
- 1/2 cup unsalted butter, melted
- 1/4 cup granulated sugar

For the Cheesecake Filling:

- 4 packages (32 ounces) cream cheese, softened
- 1 1/2 cups granulated sugar
- 4 large eggs
- 1 cup canned pumpkin puree
- 1/4 cup all-purpose flour
- 1/4 teaspoon ground cinnamon
- 1/4 teaspoon ground nutmeg
- 1/4 teaspoon ground cloves
- 1/4 teaspoon salt
- 1 teaspoon vanilla extract

For the Topping (Optional):

- Whipped cream
- Caramel sauce
- Chopped pecans or walnuts

Instructions:

Crust:

Preheat Oven:
- Preheat your oven to 325°F (163°C). Grease a 9-inch springform pan.

Make Crust:
- In a medium bowl, combine graham cracker crumbs, melted butter, and granulated sugar. Press the mixture firmly into the bottom of the prepared springform pan to form the crust.

Bake:
- Bake the crust in the preheated oven for about 10 minutes. Remove from the oven and let it cool while you prepare the filling.

Cheesecake Filling:

Beat Cream Cheese:
- In a large bowl, beat the softened cream cheese until smooth.

Add Sugar:
- Add the granulated sugar and beat until well combined.

Add Eggs:
- Add the eggs one at a time, beating well after each addition.

Add Pumpkin and Dry Ingredients:
- Add the canned pumpkin puree, flour, ground cinnamon, ground nutmeg, ground cloves, salt, and vanilla extract. Beat until smooth and well combined.

Pour Over Crust:
- Pour the pumpkin cheesecake filling over the cooled crust in the springform pan.

Bake:
- Bake in the preheated oven for 1 hour or until the center is set and the edges are slightly browned.

Cool and Refrigerate:
- Allow the pumpkin cheesecake to cool in the pan for about 10 minutes, then run a knife around the edges to loosen it. Let it cool completely on a wire rack before refrigerating for at least 4 hours or overnight.

Topping (Optional):

Serve with Whipped Cream:
- Before serving, you can top slices of pumpkin cheesecake with whipped cream.

Drizzle with Caramel and Nuts:
- Optionally, drizzle caramel sauce over the top and sprinkle with chopped pecans or walnuts.

Tips:

- Room Temperature Ingredients: Ensure that the cream cheese and eggs are at room temperature for a smoother cheesecake batter.

- Water Bath: To prevent cracks, you can bake the cheesecake in a water bath. Wrap the springform pan in foil and place it in a larger baking dish. Fill the larger dish with hot water halfway up the sides of the springform pan.

Enjoy the creamy and flavorful goodness of homemade pumpkin cheesecake – a perfect dessert for fall celebrations or any time you're craving a delicious treat!

Chocolate Pecan Tart

Ingredients:

For the Tart Crust:

- 1 1/4 cups all-purpose flour
- 1/4 cup unsweetened cocoa powder
- 1/2 cup unsalted butter, cold and cubed
- 1/4 cup granulated sugar
- 1 large egg yolk
- 2 tablespoons ice water

For the Chocolate Pecan Filling:

- 1 cup semisweet or bittersweet chocolate, chopped
- 1/2 cup heavy cream
- 1/4 cup unsalted butter
- 3 large eggs
- 1 cup granulated sugar
- 1 teaspoon vanilla extract
- 1/4 teaspoon salt
- 1 1/2 cups pecan halves

Instructions:

Tart Crust:

    Prepare the Dough:
- In a food processor, combine the flour, cocoa powder, and sugar. Add the cold, cubed butter and pulse until the mixture resembles coarse crumbs.

    Add Egg Yolk and Water:
- Add the egg yolk and ice water, and pulse until the dough comes together. Do not overmix.

    Form a Disk:
- Turn the dough out onto a lightly floured surface, gather it into a disk, wrap in plastic wrap, and refrigerate for at least 30 minutes.

    Roll Out and Fit Into Tart Pan:
- Preheat your oven to 350°F (175°C). On a floured surface, roll out the chilled dough to fit a 9-inch tart pan. Press the dough into the pan, trimming any excess.

Blind Bake:
- Line the tart crust with parchment paper and fill with pie weights or dried beans. Bake in the preheated oven for 15 minutes. Remove the weights and parchment paper and bake for an additional 5 minutes. Allow the crust to cool.

Chocolate Pecan Filling:

Preheat Oven:
- Maintain the oven temperature at 350°F (175°C).

Prepare Chocolate Ganache:
- In a heatproof bowl, combine the chopped chocolate, heavy cream, and butter. Melt the mixture over a double boiler or in the microwave, stirring until smooth. Let it cool slightly.

Mix Eggs and Sugar:
- In a separate bowl, whisk together the eggs, sugar, vanilla extract, and salt.

Combine Chocolate and Egg Mixtures:
- Slowly pour the melted chocolate mixture into the egg mixture, stirring constantly until well combined.

Add Pecans:
- Fold in the pecan halves.

Fill the Tart Shell:
- Pour the chocolate pecan filling into the pre-baked tart crust.

Bake:
- Bake in the preheated oven for 25-30 minutes or until the filling is set and slightly puffed.

Cool:
- Allow the Chocolate Pecan Tart to cool completely before slicing.

Tips:

- Chill the Dough: Chilling the tart dough ensures a flakier crust.
- Variation: You can add a splash of bourbon or rum to the filling for an extra layer of flavor.

Serve slices of this Chocolate Pecan Tart with a dollop of whipped cream or a scoop of vanilla ice cream for an indulgent and delightful dessert. Enjoy!

Desserts - Cookies:

Pumpkin Snickerdoodles

Ingredients:

For the Cookie Dough:

- 2 3/4 cups all-purpose flour
- 1 teaspoon baking soda
- 1/2 teaspoon baking powder
- 1/2 teaspoon salt
- 1 1/2 teaspoons ground cinnamon
- 1/2 teaspoon ground nutmeg
- 1/2 cup unsalted butter, softened
- 1/2 cup granulated sugar
- 1/2 cup light brown sugar, packed
- 1 cup canned pumpkin puree
- 1 large egg
- 1 teaspoon vanilla extract

For the Snickerdoodle Coating:

- 1/4 cup granulated sugar
- 1 teaspoon ground cinnamon

Instructions:

Preheat Oven:
- Preheat your oven to 350°F (175°C). Line baking sheets with parchment paper.

Whisk Dry Ingredients:
- In a medium bowl, whisk together the flour, baking soda, baking powder, salt, cinnamon, and nutmeg. Set aside.

Cream Butter and Sugars:
- In a large bowl, cream together the softened butter, granulated sugar, and brown sugar until light and fluffy.

Add Pumpkin and Egg:
- Add the pumpkin puree, egg, and vanilla extract to the creamed mixture. Mix until well combined.

Incorporate Dry Ingredients:

- Gradually add the dry ingredients to the wet ingredients, mixing just until combined. Do not overmix.

Chill Dough (Optional):
- For better results, you can chill the cookie dough in the refrigerator for 30 minutes to an hour. This helps prevent the cookies from spreading too much during baking.

Prepare Snickerdoodle Coating:
- In a small bowl, mix together the granulated sugar and cinnamon for the snickerdoodle coating.

Shape Dough Balls:
- Scoop out portions of cookie dough and roll them into 1 to 1.5-inch balls.

Coat in Cinnamon Sugar:
- Roll each dough ball in the cinnamon-sugar mixture, ensuring they are well coated.

Place on Baking Sheets:
- Place the coated dough balls on the prepared baking sheets, leaving some space between each cookie.

Flatten Slightly:
- Optionally, gently flatten each cookie with the bottom of a glass or your fingers.

Bake:
- Bake in the preheated oven for 10-12 minutes or until the edges are set. The centers may still be soft.

Cool:
- Allow the Pumpkin Snickerdoodles to cool on the baking sheets for a few minutes before transferring them to a wire rack to cool completely.

Tips:

- Pumpkin Puree: Make sure to use canned pumpkin puree, not pumpkin pie filling, for the correct flavor.

These Pumpkin Snickerdoodles are soft, chewy, and packed with warm fall spices. They make a delicious treat for autumn or any time you're in the mood for a tasty pumpkin-flavored cookie. Enjoy!

Pecan Sandies

Ingredients:

- 1 cup unsalted butter, softened
- 1/2 cup powdered sugar, plus extra for coating
- 2 teaspoons vanilla extract
- 2 cups all-purpose flour
- 1/4 teaspoon salt
- 1 cup pecans, finely chopped

Instructions:

Preheat Oven:
- Preheat your oven to 325°F (163°C). Line baking sheets with parchment paper.

Cream Butter and Sugar:
- In a large bowl, cream together the softened butter and 1/2 cup of powdered sugar until light and fluffy.

Add Vanilla Extract:
- Mix in the vanilla extract until well combined.

Combine Dry Ingredients:
- In a separate bowl, whisk together the flour and salt.

Incorporate Pecans:
- Gradually add the flour mixture to the butter mixture, mixing until just combined. Fold in the finely chopped pecans.

Shape Dough Balls:
- Scoop out portions of cookie dough and roll them into 1-inch balls. Place them on the prepared baking sheets, leaving a bit of space between each cookie.

Bake:
- Bake in the preheated oven for 12-15 minutes or until the edges are lightly golden.

Cool Slightly:
- Allow the cookies to cool on the baking sheets for a few minutes.

Coat in Powdered Sugar:
- While the cookies are still warm, roll them in powdered sugar until completely coated. You can also gently shake off any excess sugar.

Cool Completely:
- Transfer the coated cookies to a wire rack to cool completely.

Re-Coat (Optional):
- If desired, you can give the cookies a second coating of powdered sugar once they are completely cooled.

Store:
- Store the Pecan Sandies in an airtight container at room temperature.

Tips:

- Finely Chopped Pecans: For a more pronounced pecan flavor, finely chop the pecans, almost to the point of being ground.

These Pecan Sandies are perfect for holiday celebrations or any time you're craving a simple and delightful buttery cookie. Enjoy their melt-in-your-mouth goodness!

Thanksgiving Sugar Cookies

Ingredients:

For the Sugar Cookies:

- 2 3/4 cups all-purpose flour
- 1 teaspoon baking soda
- 1/2 teaspoon baking powder
- 1 cup unsalted butter, softened
- 1 1/2 cups granulated sugar
- 1 large egg
- 1 teaspoon vanilla extract
- 1/2 teaspoon almond extract (optional)
- 1/2 teaspoon salt

For Decorating:

- Royal icing
- Food coloring (in fall colors like orange, brown, yellow)
- Sprinkles or edible decorations

Instructions:

Sugar Cookies:

Preheat Oven:
- Preheat your oven to 375°F (190°C). Line baking sheets with parchment paper.

Combine Dry Ingredients:
- In a medium bowl, whisk together the flour, baking soda, baking powder, and salt. Set aside.

Cream Butter and Sugar:
- In a large bowl, cream together the softened butter and granulated sugar until light and fluffy.

Add Egg and Extracts:
- Beat in the egg, vanilla extract, and almond extract (if using) until well combined.

Incorporate Dry Ingredients:
- Gradually add the dry ingredients to the wet ingredients, mixing just until the dough comes together.

Chill Dough:
- Divide the dough into two portions, flatten each into a disk, wrap in plastic wrap, and refrigerate for at least 1 hour.

Roll Out and Cut Shapes:
- Preheat your oven again to 375°F (190°C). On a floured surface, roll out the chilled dough to about 1/4-inch thickness. Use Thanksgiving-themed cookie cutters to cut out shapes.

Bake:
- Place the cutout cookies on the prepared baking sheets and bake for 8-10 minutes or until the edges are lightly golden. Allow them to cool on the baking sheets for a few minutes before transferring to wire racks to cool completely.

Decorating:

Prepare Royal Icing:
- Mix up a batch of royal icing. Divide it into separate bowls and color each portion with your desired food coloring.

Outline and Flood:
- Use a piping bag to outline the cookies with the desired color of icing. Once the outline is set, thin the remaining icing with a bit of water to flood the inside of the outlines. Allow the icing to set.

Add Details:
- Use different colors of icing to add details, such as eyes, feathers, or pumpkin features. You can also use sprinkles or edible decorations for extra flair.

Allow Icing to Set:
- Allow the decorated cookies to sit until the icing is completely set.

Serve and Enjoy:
- Arrange your beautifully decorated Thanksgiving Sugar Cookies on a platter and serve them to your guests!

Feel free to get creative with your designs, and have fun decorating these Thanksgiving-themed sugar cookies for a festive and delicious treat!

Desserts - Cakes:

Apple Cider Cake

Ingredients:

For the Cake:

- 2 1/2 cups all-purpose flour
- 2 teaspoons baking powder
- 1/2 teaspoon baking soda
- 1/2 teaspoon salt
- 1 teaspoon ground cinnamon
- 1/2 teaspoon ground nutmeg
- 1 cup unsalted butter, softened
- 1 cup granulated sugar
- 1/2 cup brown sugar, packed
- 3 large eggs
- 1 teaspoon vanilla extract
- 1 cup apple cider

For the Glaze:

- 1/2 cup apple cider
- 1/4 cup unsalted butter
- 1 cup confectioners' sugar
- 1/2 teaspoon vanilla extract
- Pinch of salt

Instructions:

For the Cake:

    Preheat Oven:
- Preheat your oven to 350°F (175°C). Grease and flour a bundt pan.

    Whisk Dry Ingredients:
- In a medium bowl, whisk together the flour, baking powder, baking soda, salt, cinnamon, and nutmeg. Set aside.

    Cream Butter and Sugars:
- In a large bowl, cream together the softened butter, granulated sugar, and brown sugar until light and fluffy.

Add Eggs and Vanilla:
- Add the eggs one at a time, beating well after each addition. Mix in the vanilla extract.

Alternate Additions:
- Gradually add the dry ingredients to the wet ingredients in three parts, alternating with the apple cider. Begin and end with the dry ingredients. Mix until just combined.

Pour into Bundt Pan:
- Pour the batter into the prepared bundt pan, spreading it evenly.

Bake:
- Bake in the preheated oven for 45-50 minutes or until a toothpick inserted into the center comes out clean.

Cool:
- Allow the cake to cool in the pan for 15 minutes, then transfer it to a wire rack to cool completely.

For the Glaze:

Combine Glaze Ingredients:
- In a small saucepan, combine the apple cider and butter. Bring to a simmer over medium heat, stirring occasionally, until the butter is melted.

Add Confectioners' Sugar and Vanilla:
- Remove from heat and whisk in the confectioners' sugar, vanilla extract, and a pinch of salt until smooth.

Glaze the Cake:
- Pour the warm glaze over the cooled cake, allowing it to drizzle down the sides. Let the glaze set before serving.

Tips:

- Warm Glaze: For a more pronounced apple cider flavor, you can use warm glaze on a cooled cake.

This Apple Cider Cake is a perfect addition to your fall and Thanksgiving dessert table, offering a moist and flavorful treat that captures the essence of autumn. Enjoy!

Maple Pecan Cake

Ingredients:

For the Cake:

- 2 1/2 cups all-purpose flour
- 2 1/2 teaspoons baking powder
- 1/2 teaspoon baking soda
- 1/2 teaspoon salt
- 1 cup unsalted butter, softened
- 1 cup granulated sugar
- 1 cup pure maple syrup
- 4 large eggs
- 1 teaspoon vanilla extract
- 1 cup buttermilk

For the Maple Pecan Frosting:

- 1 cup unsalted butter, softened
- 1/2 cup pure maple syrup
- 4 cups confectioners' sugar
- 1 teaspoon vanilla extract
- 1/2 cup chopped pecans, toasted (for garnish)

Instructions:

For the Cake:

> Preheat Oven:
> - Preheat your oven to 350°F (175°C). Grease and flour two 9-inch round cake pans.
>
> Whisk Dry Ingredients:
> - In a medium bowl, whisk together the flour, baking powder, baking soda, and salt. Set aside.
>
> Cream Butter and Sugar:
> - In a large bowl, cream together the softened butter and granulated sugar until light and fluffy.
>
> Add Maple Syrup:
> - Add the pure maple syrup to the butter mixture and beat until well combined.
>
> Add Eggs and Vanilla:

- Add the eggs one at a time, beating well after each addition. Mix in the vanilla extract.

Alternate Additions:
- Gradually add the dry ingredients to the wet ingredients in three parts, alternating with the buttermilk. Begin and end with the dry ingredients. Mix until just combined.

Divide Batter and Bake:
- Divide the batter evenly between the prepared cake pans. Smooth the tops with a spatula. Bake in the preheated oven for 25-30 minutes or until a toothpick inserted into the center comes out clean.

Cool:
- Allow the cakes to cool in the pans for 10 minutes, then transfer them to a wire rack to cool completely.

For the Maple Pecan Frosting:

Beat Butter:
- In a large bowl, beat the softened butter until creamy.

Add Maple Syrup and Vanilla:
- Add the pure maple syrup and vanilla extract to the butter. Beat until well combined.

Gradually Add Confectioners' Sugar:
- Gradually add the confectioners' sugar, one cup at a time, beating well after each addition until the frosting is smooth and fluffy.

Assemble the Cake:
- Place one cake layer on a serving plate. Spread a layer of maple pecan frosting over the top. Place the second cake layer on top and frost the top and sides of the entire cake.

Garnish with Toasted Pecans:
- Sprinkle the chopped pecans over the top of the frosted cake as a garnish. You can also press chopped pecans onto the sides of the cake if desired.

Slice and Serve:
- Slice and serve the Maple Pecan Cake, and enjoy the rich, flavorful goodness!

Tips:

- Toasting Pecans: Toasting the pecans adds depth of flavor. Simply place chopped pecans in a dry skillet over medium heat, stirring frequently until fragrant and lightly browned.

This Maple Pecan Cake is a wonderful choice for autumn celebrations or any time you want to indulge in a delightful and comforting dessert. Enjoy!

Drinks:

Spiced Apple Cider

Ingredients:

- 8 cups (64 ounces) apple cider
- 2 cinnamon sticks
- 4-6 whole cloves
- 4-6 whole allspice berries
- 1 orange, thinly sliced
- 1-2 tablespoons brown sugar or honey (optional, to taste)
- Optional garnish: Cinnamon sticks, orange slices, or apple slices

Instructions:

Combine Ingredients:
- In a large pot, combine the apple cider, cinnamon sticks, whole cloves, and whole allspice berries.

Add Orange Slices:
- Add the thinly sliced orange to the pot. If you like, you can also squeeze some juice from the orange into the cider for extra flavor.

Sweeten (Optional):
- If you prefer a sweeter cider, add brown sugar or honey to taste. Start with 1-2 tablespoons and adjust according to your preference.

Warm the Cider:
- Place the pot over medium heat and slowly bring the cider to a simmer. Do not boil; simmering allows the spices to infuse the cider without reducing its volume.

Simmer:
- Once the cider reaches a simmer, reduce the heat to low and let it simmer for at least 15-20 minutes. The longer it simmers, the more the flavors will meld.

Strain (Optional):
- If you prefer a smoother cider, you can strain out the spices and orange slices before serving. Otherwise, leave them in for a more rustic presentation.

Serve:

- Ladle the spiced apple cider into mugs. Optionally, garnish with cinnamon sticks, orange slices, or apple slices.

Enjoy:

- Serve the Spiced Apple Cider warm and enjoy the cozy, comforting flavors.

Tips:

- Customize Spices: Feel free to adjust the spices to your liking. You can also add a star anise or a dash of ground nutmeg for extra warmth.

This Spiced Apple Cider is a wonderful beverage to serve during chilly weather, holidays, or any time you want a comforting and aromatic drink. Enjoy the delightful flavors of fall!

Cranberry Orange Punch

Ingredients:

- 4 cups cranberry juice
- 2 cups orange juice
- 1 cup pineapple juice
- 1 liter ginger ale, chilled
- 1 orange, thinly sliced
- Fresh cranberries (for garnish, optional)
- Ice cubes

Instructions:

Combine Juices:
- In a large punch bowl or pitcher, combine the cranberry juice, orange juice, and pineapple juice.

Chill Ingredients:
- Make sure all the juices are well-chilled before preparing the punch.

Add Ginger Ale:
- Just before serving, pour the chilled ginger ale into the punch bowl or pitcher. The ginger ale adds a sparkling and effervescent quality to the punch.

Add Orange Slices:
- Add thinly sliced orange rounds to the punch for extra flavor and a decorative touch.

Garnish (Optional):
- If desired, add fresh cranberries to the punch for a festive garnish.

Serve Cold:
- Stir the punch gently to mix the ingredients. Serve the Cranberry Orange Punch over ice cubes in individual glasses.

Enjoy:
- Enjoy this refreshing and vibrant Cranberry Orange Punch with friends and family!

Tips:

- Adjust Sweetness: Depending on your taste preferences, you can add a bit of honey or simple syrup to sweeten the punch if needed.

- Frozen Fruit: Instead of ice cubes, you can use frozen cranberries or orange slices to keep the punch cold without diluting it.

This Cranberry Orange Punch is a delightful addition to holiday parties, brunches, or any occasion where you want a flavorful and festive drink. Cheers!

Leftovers:

Turkey Pot Pie

Ingredients:

For the Filling:

- 3 cups cooked turkey, shredded or diced
- 2 tablespoons unsalted butter
- 1 onion, diced
- 2 carrots, diced
- 2 celery stalks, diced
- 1 cup frozen peas
- 1/3 cup all-purpose flour
- 1/2 teaspoon salt
- 1/4 teaspoon black pepper
- 1/2 teaspoon dried thyme
- 1/2 teaspoon dried sage
- 2 cups turkey or chicken broth
- 1 cup milk

For the Pie Crust:

- 2 store-bought pie crusts or homemade if preferred

Instructions:

Preparing the Filling:

    Preheat Oven:
- Preheat your oven to 425°F (220°C).

    Saute Vegetables:
- In a large skillet, melt the butter over medium heat. Add the diced onion, carrots, and celery. Cook until the vegetables are softened, about 5-7 minutes.

    Add Flour and Seasonings:
- Sprinkle the flour over the vegetables and stir to combine. Cook for an additional 1-2 minutes to remove the raw flour taste. Add the salt, black pepper, dried thyme, and dried sage. Stir well.

Add Broth and Milk:
- Gradually add the turkey or chicken broth, stirring continuously to avoid lumps. Once the broth is incorporated, pour in the milk and continue stirring until the mixture thickens.

Add Turkey and Peas:
- Add the shredded or diced turkey and frozen peas to the skillet. Stir until the ingredients are well combined. Remove the skillet from heat.

Assembling the Pie:

Roll Out Pie Crusts:
- Roll out one pie crust and line a deep-dish pie plate with it. Trim any excess crust hanging over the edges.

Add Filling:
- Pour the turkey and vegetable filling into the pie crust-lined dish, spreading it evenly.

Cover with Second Crust:
- Roll out the second pie crust and place it over the filling. Trim and crimp the edges to seal the pie. Cut a few slits in the top crust to allow steam to escape.

Bake:
- Place the pie on a baking sheet to catch any drips. Bake in the preheated oven for 30-35 minutes or until the crust is golden brown and the filling is bubbly.

Cool and Serve:
- Allow the Turkey Pot Pie to cool for a few minutes before slicing and serving.

Tips:

- Homemade Pie Crust: If you prefer, you can make your own pie crust from scratch.
- Vegetable Variations: Feel free to add other vegetables like corn, green beans, or mushrooms to the filling.

This Turkey Pot Pie is a wonderful way to transform leftovers into a comforting meal that the whole family will enjoy. It's a classic dish that captures the essence of home-cooked comfort food.

Thanksgiving Leftover Sandwich

Ingredients:

- Sliced leftover turkey
- Stuffing
- Cranberry sauce
- Mashed potatoes
- Gravy
- Sliced bread or rolls

Instructions:

Toast Bread or Rolls (Optional):
- If you like, you can toast the bread or rolls for added texture.

Layer Mashed Potatoes:
- Start by spreading a layer of mashed potatoes on one side of the bread or roll.

Add Stuffing:
- Next, add a layer of stuffing on top of the mashed potatoes.

Layer Turkey:
- Arrange slices of leftover turkey over the stuffing.

Drizzle Gravy:
- Drizzle some warm gravy over the turkey. This adds moisture and enhances the flavors.

Dollop Cranberry Sauce:
- Add a dollop of cranberry sauce on top. The sweetness of the cranberry sauce complements the savory elements.

Top with Bread or Roll:
- Place another slice of bread or the top half of the roll to complete the sandwich.

Press and Enjoy:
- Gently press the sandwich together and enjoy your Thanksgiving Leftover Sandwich!

Variations:

- Cheese: If you like, you can add a slice of your favorite cheese, such as cheddar or Swiss.
- Greens: For freshness, add some arugula, spinach, or leftover green beans.

- Mayo or Mustard: Spread a thin layer of mayonnaise or mustard on the bread for extra flavor.

Feel free to get creative and add your favorite Thanksgiving leftovers to make a sandwich that suits your taste. It's a delightful way to enjoy the holiday flavors in a new and satisfying way!

Miscellaneous:

Homemade Grilled Turkey Stock

Ingredients:

- Leftover turkey carcass (picked mostly clean)
- 1 large onion, quartered (with skin on)
- 2 carrots, chopped
- 2 celery stalks, chopped
- 3-4 garlic cloves, smashed
- 1 tablespoon olive oil
- 1 bay leaf
- 1 teaspoon whole black peppercorns
- Fresh herbs (such as parsley, thyme, or rosemary)
- Water (enough to cover the ingredients)

Instructions:

Prepare the Turkey Carcass:
- Break the leftover turkey carcass into manageable pieces. Remove excess meat, but it's okay to leave some for added flavor.

Preheat the Grill:
- Preheat your grill to medium-high heat.

Grill the Turkey Carcass:
- Brush the turkey carcass pieces with olive oil and place them directly on the preheated grill. Grill for about 15-20 minutes, turning occasionally until the carcass pieces get a nice char and smoky flavor.

Prepare the Stock Pot:
- In a large stockpot, combine the grilled turkey carcass, quartered onion (with skin), chopped carrots, chopped celery, smashed garlic cloves, bay leaf, peppercorns, and fresh herbs.

Cover with Water:
- Pour enough water into the pot to cover all the ingredients.

Simmer the Stock:
- Bring the mixture to a boil over high heat, then reduce the heat to low. Let it simmer uncovered for at least 2-3 hours, occasionally skimming off any foam that rises to the top.

Strain the Stock:

- Once the stock has simmered and developed rich flavors, strain it through a fine-mesh strainer or cheesecloth into another large pot or bowl. Discard the solids.

Cool and Store:
- Allow the turkey stock to cool to room temperature before refrigerating or freezing. Once cooled, store it in airtight containers.

Use in Recipes:
- Use the homemade grilled turkey stock as a base for soups, stews, risotto, or any recipe that calls for flavorful stock.

Tips:

- Vegetable Scraps: Don't hesitate to use vegetable scraps like onion skins, carrot peels, and celery ends in the stock for added flavor.
- Storage: Homemade turkey stock can be stored in the refrigerator for a few days or frozen for an extended period. Make sure to leave some space in the containers for expansion if freezing.

Homemade Grilled Turkey Stock adds a smoky depth of flavor to your recipes, making it a worthwhile endeavor with your Thanksgiving leftovers.

Candied Sweet Potatoes

Ingredients:

- 4-5 medium-sized sweet potatoes, peeled and sliced into rounds or cubes
- 1/2 cup unsalted butter, melted
- 1/2 cup brown sugar
- 1/4 cup maple syrup or honey
- 1 teaspoon ground cinnamon
- 1/2 teaspoon ground nutmeg
- 1/2 teaspoon vanilla extract
- 1/2 teaspoon salt
- Chopped pecans or marshmallows for topping (optional)

Instructions:

Preheat Oven:
- Preheat your oven to 375°F (190°C).

Prepare Sweet Potatoes:
- Peel the sweet potatoes and slice them into rounds or cubes, about 1/4 to 1/2 inch thick.

Mix Candied Coating:
- In a large bowl, combine the melted butter, brown sugar, maple syrup or honey, ground cinnamon, ground nutmeg, vanilla extract, and salt. Stir until the ingredients are well combined.

Coat Sweet Potatoes:
- Add the sweet potato slices or cubes to the bowl with the candied coating. Toss until the sweet potatoes are evenly coated.

Layer in Baking Dish:
- Transfer the coated sweet potatoes to a greased baking dish, spreading them out into an even layer.

Bake:
- Bake in the preheated oven for 40-45 minutes or until the sweet potatoes are tender, stirring halfway through the baking time.

Optional Toppings:
- If you like, you can add chopped pecans or marshmallows during the last 10 minutes of baking for an extra layer of flavor and texture.

Serve:
- Once the sweet potatoes are tender and caramelized, remove them from the oven. Let them cool for a few minutes before serving.

Tips:

- Uniform Slices: Try to cut the sweet potatoes into uniform slices or cubes to ensure even cooking.
- Adjust Sweetness: Taste the candied coating before tossing it with the sweet potatoes and adjust the sweetness to your liking.

Candied Sweet Potatoes are a wonderful side dish that perfectly balances the natural sweetness of sweet potatoes with warm spices. They make a great addition to your holiday table or any special meal. Enjoy!

Breakfast/Brunch:

Pumpkin Pancakes

Ingredients:

- 1 cup all-purpose flour
- 2 tablespoons brown sugar
- 1 teaspoon baking powder
- 1/2 teaspoon baking soda
- 1/2 teaspoon ground cinnamon
- 1/4 teaspoon ground nutmeg
- 1/4 teaspoon ground ginger
- 1/4 teaspoon salt
- 3/4 cup buttermilk
- 1/2 cup pumpkin puree
- 1 large egg
- 2 tablespoons unsalted butter, melted
- 1 teaspoon vanilla extract
- Butter or oil for cooking
- Maple syrup and whipped cream for serving

Instructions:

Preheat Griddle or Pan:
- Preheat a griddle or non-stick pan over medium heat.

Combine Dry Ingredients:
- In a large bowl, whisk together the flour, brown sugar, baking powder, baking soda, ground cinnamon, nutmeg, ginger, and salt.

Mix Wet Ingredients:
- In another bowl, whisk together the buttermilk, pumpkin puree, egg, melted butter, and vanilla extract.

Combine Wet and Dry Ingredients:
- Pour the wet ingredients into the dry ingredients and gently stir until just combined. Do not overmix; it's okay if there are a few lumps.

Cook Pancakes:
- Grease the griddle or pan with butter or oil. Spoon the batter onto the griddle to form pancakes of your desired size.

Cook Until Bubbles Form:

- Cook until bubbles form on the surface of the pancakes and the edges begin to set, usually about 2-3 minutes.

Flip and Cook:
- Flip the pancakes with a spatula and cook for an additional 1-2 minutes on the other side, or until golden brown.

Serve:
- Transfer the pancakes to a plate, and repeat with the remaining batter. Serve the Pumpkin Pancakes warm with maple syrup and whipped cream.

Tips:

- Keep Warm: If you're making a batch, you can keep the cooked pancakes warm in a preheated oven (200°F or 93°C) while you finish cooking the rest.
- Add-ins: Consider adding chopped nuts, chocolate chips, or dried cranberries to the batter for extra flavor and texture.

Pumpkin Pancakes are a delightful way to start your day with the warm and comforting flavors of fall. Enjoy them with your favorite toppings for a delicious breakfast treat!

Thanksgiving Breakfast Casserole

Ingredients:

- 8 slices of bread, cubed
- 1 pound breakfast sausage, cooked and crumbled
- 1 cup shredded cheddar cheese
- 1 cup shredded mozzarella cheese
- 1 cup diced cooked turkey (leftover from Thanksgiving)
- 1/2 cup diced bell peppers (assorted colors)
- 1/2 cup diced onion
- 8 large eggs
- 2 cups milk
- 1 teaspoon Dijon mustard
- 1/2 teaspoon dried sage
- Salt and pepper to taste
- Chopped fresh parsley for garnish (optional)

Instructions:

Preheat Oven:
- Preheat your oven to 350°F (175°C). Grease a 9x13-inch baking dish.

Prepare Bread Base:
- Place the cubed bread in the prepared baking dish.

Layer Sausage and Cheeses:
- Sprinkle the cooked and crumbled sausage over the bread cubes. Follow with a layer of shredded cheddar and mozzarella cheeses.

Add Turkey and Vegetables:
- Sprinkle the diced cooked turkey over the cheese layer. Add diced bell peppers and onions evenly over the casserole.

Whisk Egg Mixture:
- In a large bowl, whisk together the eggs, milk, Dijon mustard, dried sage, salt, and pepper.

Pour Egg Mixture:
- Pour the egg mixture evenly over the casserole, ensuring all ingredients are well-coated.

Allow to Soak:
- Press down slightly on the ingredients to allow the bread to soak up the egg mixture. Let it sit for about 10-15 minutes to allow the bread to absorb the liquid.

Bake:
- Bake in the preheated oven for 45-50 minutes or until the top is golden brown, and the casserole is set in the center.

Garnish and Serve:
- If desired, garnish with chopped fresh parsley before serving. Allow the casserole to cool for a few minutes before slicing and serving.

Tips:

- Make-Ahead Option: You can prepare the casserole the night before, cover it, and refrigerate. Bake it in the morning for a convenient make-ahead breakfast.
- Customize Ingredients: Feel free to add other Thanksgiving leftovers like roasted vegetables, cranberry sauce, or different cheeses.

This Thanksgiving Breakfast Casserole is a hearty and flavorful way to kick off your holiday celebrations. It's a versatile recipe that allows you to incorporate your favorite Thanksgiving ingredients into a delicious morning meal.

Extras:

Homemade Cranberry Butter

Ingredients:

- 1 cup unsalted butter, softened
- 1/2 cup cranberry sauce (homemade or store-bought)
- 2 tablespoons powdered sugar (adjust to taste)
- 1/2 teaspoon vanilla extract (optional)

Instructions:

- Prepare Cranberry Sauce (if not using store-bought):
    - If you don't have store-bought cranberry sauce, you can make a quick version by simmering fresh or frozen cranberries with sugar and a bit of water until they burst and the mixture thickens. Let it cool before using.
- Combine Ingredients:
    - In a mixing bowl, combine the softened butter, cranberry sauce, powdered sugar, and vanilla extract (if using).
- Beat Until Smooth:
    - Use a hand mixer or stand mixer to beat the ingredients together until smooth and well combined. Scrape down the sides of the bowl to ensure all ingredients are incorporated.
- Adjust Sweetness:
    - Taste the cranberry butter and adjust the sweetness by adding more powdered sugar if needed. Keep in mind that the sweetness will also depend on the sweetness of your cranberry sauce.
- Chill (Optional):
    - If the cranberry butter is too soft, you can refrigerate it for about 30 minutes to firm it up slightly.
- Serve:
    - Transfer the Cranberry Butter to a jar or bowl. It's ready to be served!

Serving Ideas:

- Spread on Toast or Bagels: Enjoy Cranberry Butter on warm toast, bagels, or English muffins for a delicious and festive breakfast.
- Top Pancakes or Waffles: Add a dollop of Cranberry Butter to your pancakes or waffles for a burst of flavor.

- Muffin or Scone Spread: Use it as a delightful spread for muffins or scones.

Tips:

- Experiment with Flavors: Consider adding a pinch of orange zest or a splash of orange juice for an additional layer of flavor.
- Make Ahead: Cranberry Butter can be made ahead of time and stored in the refrigerator. Allow it to come to room temperature before serving.

Homemade Cranberry Butter is a wonderful addition to your holiday table, bringing the sweet and tangy flavors of cranberries to your breakfast or brunch. Enjoy the festive goodness!

Homemade Dinner Rolls

Ingredients:

- 4 to 4 1/2 cups all-purpose flour
- 1/4 cup granulated sugar
- 1 tablespoon active dry yeast
- 1 teaspoon salt
- 1 cup warm milk (110°F or 43°C)
- 1/4 cup unsalted butter, melted
- 1 large egg

Instructions:

Activate Yeast:
- In a small bowl, combine warm milk and a pinch of sugar. Sprinkle the yeast over the milk and let it sit for about 5-10 minutes until it becomes frothy.

Mix Dry Ingredients:
- In a large mixing bowl, combine 4 cups of flour, sugar, and salt.

Add Wet Ingredients:
- Make a well in the center of the dry ingredients. Pour in the activated yeast mixture, melted butter, and beaten egg.

Knead Dough:
- Mix the ingredients until a dough forms. Turn the dough onto a floured surface and knead for about 8-10 minutes, adding more flour as needed, until the dough is smooth and elastic.

First Rise:
- Place the dough in a greased bowl, cover it with a damp cloth or plastic wrap, and let it rise in a warm place for about 1-1.5 hours or until it doubles in size.

Punch Down and Shape:
- Once the dough has risen, punch it down, and turn it out onto a floured surface. Divide the dough into equal-sized portions and shape them into rolls.

Second Rise:
- Place the shaped rolls in a greased baking dish or on a baking sheet, leaving some space between each roll. Cover and let them rise for another 30-45 minutes.

Preheat Oven:

- Preheat your oven to 375°F (190°C).

Bake:
- Bake the rolls in the preheated oven for 12-15 minutes or until they are golden brown on top.

Brush with Butter (Optional):
- Brush the tops of the rolls with melted butter immediately after taking them out of the oven for a glossy finish.

Cool and Serve:
- Allow the dinner rolls to cool for a few minutes before serving.

Tips:

- Check Yeast Freshness: Make sure your yeast is fresh. If it doesn't become frothy during activation, it may be inactive.
- Butter on Top: Brushing the baked rolls with melted butter gives them a shiny finish and adds extra flavor.

These Homemade Dinner Rolls are perfect for any occasion, especially holiday dinners. Serve them warm with butter, and they are sure to be a hit at your table!

Caramel Apple Cheesecake Bars

Ingredients:

For the Crust:

- 1 1/2 cups graham cracker crumbs
- 1/2 cup unsalted butter, melted
- 1/4 cup granulated sugar

For the Cheesecake Filling:

- 16 ounces (2 blocks) cream cheese, softened
- 1/2 cup granulated sugar
- 2 large eggs
- 1 teaspoon vanilla extract

For the Apple Layer:

- 2 medium-sized apples, peeled, cored, and finely chopped
- 1 tablespoon lemon juice
- 1/4 cup granulated sugar
- 1/2 teaspoon ground cinnamon
- 1/4 teaspoon ground nutmeg

For the Caramel Topping:

- 1/2 cup caramel sauce (store-bought or homemade)

Instructions:

Preheat Oven:
- Preheat your oven to 350°F (175°C). Grease a 9x9-inch baking pan or line it with parchment paper, leaving an overhang for easy removal.

Make the Crust:
- In a bowl, combine graham cracker crumbs, melted butter, and sugar. Press the mixture firmly into the bottom of the prepared baking pan to create the crust.

Prepare Apple Layer:
- In a separate bowl, toss the finely chopped apples with lemon juice, sugar, cinnamon, and nutmeg until the apples are evenly coated. Spread the apple mixture over the crust.

Make the Cheesecake Filling:
- In a large mixing bowl, beat the softened cream cheese until smooth. Add sugar, eggs, and vanilla extract, and continue to beat until well combined. Pour the cheesecake filling over the apple layer.

Bake:
- Bake in the preheated oven for 35-40 minutes or until the edges are set, and the center is slightly jiggly. The cheesecake will continue to set as it cools.

Cool and Chill:
- Allow the Caramel Apple Cheesecake Bars to cool completely in the pan, then refrigerate for at least 3 hours or overnight to allow the flavors to meld.

Drizzle with Caramel:
- Before serving, drizzle caramel sauce over the chilled cheesecake bars.

Slice and Serve:
- Use the parchment paper overhang to lift the cheesecake out of the pan. Slice into bars and serve.

Tips:

- Variation: Consider adding a sprinkle of chopped nuts, such as pecans or walnuts, over the caramel topping for added crunch.
- Caramel Sauce: You can use store-bought caramel sauce or make your own by melting caramels or combining sweetened condensed milk with butter.

These Caramel Apple Cheesecake Bars are a delightful blend of creamy cheesecake, spiced apples, and sweet caramel. They make a wonderful fall or holiday dessert that will impress your family and friends. Enjoy!

www.ingramcontent.com/pod-product-compliance
Lightning Source LLC
LaVergne TN
LVHW081605060526
838201LV00054B/2092